T.J. Humphries wrote this book following the suicide of his youngest daughter at the age of 28 after her suffering a harrowing decade of mental health issues and depression.

His words are designed to help parents in a similar position who feel it impossible to believe that, one day, there may be light at the end of the tunnel.

And those parents who may not realise that God is walking with them every step of the way along that tunnel.

T.J. Humphries

THE LONG ROAD TO FREEDOM

AUSTIN MACAULEY PUBLISHERS™

LONDON • CAMBRIDGE • NEW YORK • SHARJAH

A CIP catalogue record for this title is available from the British
Library.

ISBN 9781398490437 (Paperback)
ISBN 9781398490444 (ePub e-book)

www.austinmacauley.com

First Published 2023
Austin Macauley Publishers Ltd®
1 Canada Square
Canary Wharf
London
E14 5AA

Foreword

People in my position must often ask themselves what the answer is. How did I get here? At what cost?

And how did I finally come out on the other side, into a world where the grass is green and smells fresh. Where life is worth living and relishing for every last facet of its existence – a place where utopia can exist for the simplest of men.

It is ironic that what finally triggered my debut book was being handed the psychiatric report on our youngest daughter's suicide.

People always say that inside every good journalist is a book, and I always joked that that ruled me out in that case.

But what I discovered in writing this is that I was happily transported back to the days when I wrote my finest articles over a long career in the written word at a number of respected newspapers across the north of the country and in the Midlands.

On those occasions I simply held my hands above the keys, and God did the rest – in what was pretty much a joint effort. Though, I must admit, it seemed that very little contribution came from me.

So I would like to take this opportunity to thank my mate, God (it's not what you know), in assisting me to pen my first ever book and helping me to write what I feel, on reflection, is the most important thing that I have ever put to paper.

Especially if it mends the heart of the woman I love, because she deserves to find peace and contentment in my world that she has played such a massive part in shaping.

I never knew what people would be interested in about me and my family. My life in and around the edges of sport at the very highest level; my complicated growing up though adoption and the struggles that ensued – I overheard my aunty say at a funeral: "Isn't it amazing how he ended up normal?" I didn't. Or simply how life panned out in general.

But then I thought about what everyone is looking for – the secret of a happy life. And this story is about the journey that it took to get there.

And my wife, Maria, and I are still on that journey, trying to piece our lives back together after losing our precious youngest daughter in the most tragic of circumstances.

We will never be able to bring her back. Obviously. But we can take massive strides towards rebuilding a family that was once so strong, and bringing it back to a time when laughter really was the most valuable thing we had.

You will laugh and you will cry in equal measure, and hopefully somewhere along the way, you will be inspired. But what you could not do, no matter how you tried, is make any of this stuff up.

Chapter One
The Beginning

I WAS the result of a shag at a party in 1959. Headingley in Leeds is a student area where parties, alcohol and parent-free attitudes lead to a more relaxed ambience of an evening.

There is every chance that my biological dad doesn't have a clue that I exist – in fact, there is every chance that he is dead given that I was 61 when I decided to open the keyboard on these memoirs.

But fortunately, my mother was a Roman Catholic, and when she discovered that her fun evening was to have life-altering consequences, she elected to keep me and eventually give birth in an orphanage in Headingley and hand over my care to the Catholic Church.

I never found out who my 'real' mum and dad were, but 25 years later, I did revisit the orphanage with my dad (my adopted father) and spent a very moving time there in search of my roots.

As I say, my biological father probably left the party no wiser and chuffed with another notch on his belt, but I do think of my biological mother on my birthday (June 13th) every year and feel her sadness. As a parent and a grandparent myself now, I can understand how she must feel each passing year. If she, indeed, is still with us.

The priest who welcomed us to the orphanage came up with the opening gambit of: "Welcome back, Simon." So I suppose he could have broken it a bit easier, but I always think, as a Yorkshire lad, it is best to have these things out in the open.

Apparently, my birth mother's other major contribution was to name me Simon John. When I was officially adopted at seven months old, my new mum and dad named me Timothy and kept the John bit, and I was wrapped up to be shipped off to Bradford.

Chapter Two
The Loony Bin

WHEN football chairmen are considered whether they are suitable to be in charge of professional football clubs, they have to pass what is known as 'the fit and proper persons act'. Which basically means they have to prove that they have a lot of money. Oodles and oodles of the stuff.

I worked for the chairman of a football club in my now adopted home town of Monkstone, and we thought that he had a lot of money, but it didn't take long for it to run out. And, when it did, the dreams of footballing glory for our little slice of the Midlands died with it.

My adopted mum was a lovely, caring lady, who unfortunately suffered from severe mental health problems, and that eventually led me to being farmed out again between the ages of three and four while she spent some time in a mental institution.

I was never allowed to call it a 'loony bin' – not at the time, obviously, because that would have been considered a bit callous even as a Yorkshire three-year-old – but the padded wallpaper was a bit of a clue.

I loved her to bits, but the 'fit and proper persons act' might have found her, as a mother, in the same league as potential football chairmen.

Still, we got through it. I went on to gain the nearest thing to a sister that I ever had, and we even managed to brush off the brief blip where my new mother attempted to strangle my new father.

Chapter Three
Carmel

WHILE my mother got used to living with wallpaper that you could bounce off, I went from being an only child to living in a house in Leeds which contained my dad's sister and her husband and their five sons and daughters, and my father's mother.

David and Elaine were the oldest. Benjamin tolerated me and taught me chess and then battered me at it. John knocked off my spoiled brat edges, and Carmel (who was four) took me under her wing.

Beds were obviously at a premium, and while I started off in a cot in my uncle John and aunty's bedroom, I was later promoted to sleeping in the girls' room, where I shared a single bed with Carmel. All went well, despite the early teething problems which emerged when I was allowed to sleep in my vest and she wasn't.

Carmel was left-handed and she was my hero. She was brilliant at everything and, we were inseparable. Even when I eventually went back to Bradford, the highlights of my weekends in Leeds were when she ran into the sitting room, and greeted me with: "How's my favourite cousin?"

Christmas Days in Bradford were always rushed through so that I could spend Boxing Day at my cousins' house playing endless board games around the massive dining table.

Carmel was outstanding in every subject at school and was a straight shoo-in to Oxford or Cambridge, but when she was 17, she went on holiday to France and fell in love with Paul. After a whirlwind romance, they got married while she was there but, despite the fact that they were clearly so very much in love, the grown-ups in the family took it very badly and said that it was a waste of such a promising life – whereas we kids admired her for living a fairy tale.

Six months later, I came home from school in Bradford one Thursday evening and noticed that there was a sombre atmosphere in the house.

As ever when there was something serious afoot, my mum said: "There's someone we need to say a prayer for."

It turned out that Helen had leukaemia. By Saturday, she was dead.

I had just started learning how to play the guitar. I charged out of the house and ran as fast as I could for miles and miles, with no particular place to go – just howling at the wind and shouting all the names under the sun at God through my tears.

When I returned home, I sat down and wrote the following song – just something that her husband may have written himself:-

TO BE NICE

'She was always asking questions, to which the answers always lay so deep, and in her sleep,

'She'd ask me if I noticed any difference in the way that I'd kiss her goodnight, or said sleep tight,

'And she asked me if I loved her, or was I merely joking, or was I really saying it to be nice.

'She said when she was older she'd like to settle down and have a child, so undefiled, so undefiled,

'She told me to burn my schoolbooks, and to go and live with her and we'd fly like kites, it'd be oh so nice,

'And she asked me if I loved her, or was I merely joking, or was I really saying it to be nice.

'But I never knew the secret she was hiding deep inside, and the day she died, well I really cried,

'Cos I'd burnt all of my schoolbooks and I'd gone and lived with her and we'd flown like kites, it was oh so nice,

'And then she'd asked me if I loved her, or was I merely joking, or was I really saying it to be nice.'

Chapter Four
School Days

I WENT to Bradford Grammar School in the early 1970s when it was one of the top three schools in the whole of the country.

The rugby coach was the England Under-18 Rugby coach, etc., etc. It was £700 a term back then and 75% of the kids got picked up by their gardeners in the family's Rolls Royces at lunchtime.

The other 25% of us passed our entrance exams after having the formative years of our childhood ruined by parental enforced studying for the bloody things.

Anyway, passing the entrance exam was right up there with the first wank and I was in.

In the first few months, I met this lad called Fred Hubbard who was right on my wavelength. He was a rough Yorkshire diamond from a farm just outside Bradford and we became firm friends for life (of which mine in particular he would play a starring role in extending).

For the next seven years, I either stayed at his house or he was at my house and we grew up together and fell in and out of love (sometimes with the same girl) and generally he became my brother much in the same way as my late 'sister' Carmel.

As Yorkshire men, we don't tell each other that we love each other, but he doesn't need to read this book to know that that's a fact.

And he wouldn't have driven for two hours at two minutes' notice in answer to my text 'Help. I'm struggling' if that wasn't reciprocated.

But school life wasn't for me, and I realised that the usual fast-track to either Cambridge or Oxford universities wasn't to be the end result of my Bradford Grammar School days. Fortunately the headmaster was a remarkable man.

I was summoned to his grand office, and was welcomed into its rich polished oak interior with the words: "Come in, Smith, take a seat."

I expected the Eastenders drums at that point, but what I got what an example of teaching master craft at the very highest level.

"Tell me, Smith," he intoned. "Why are you fucking about at your exams?"

Jesus Christ!! This man knows the words we use! It was sheer genius. Straight away, he had the undivided attention of a gob-smacked 18-year-old who was ready to hang on his every word.

"You're not going to pass your A-Levels. But I love the way you write. My friend is the editor on the local paper. You'll start in September."

Chapter Five
Journalism

THE Telegragh and Argus has been the evening paper in Bradford since Methuselah was a cub reporter.

And I was thrown into the adult world pretty sharpish. My Saturday night before that point was: up the hill to Aunty Jane's house; Kojak; Match of the Day; glass of milk; bed. First Monday at work at the Telegraph was: introduced to work colleagues; typing up wedding reports; across the road to the Queen's Head for six pints of bitter; then, I believe, back to work for some more wedding reports. Possibly.

It was more or less like that for the next 40 years. With a bit of football and cricket thrown into the mix.

It took a bit of time to break on to the sports pages. They were, quite rightly, like closely guarded secrets. The Bradford City man, Bradford Northern rugby man, Yorkshire cricket correspondent, et al, were all household names who will forever be written into the pages of West Yorkshire folklore, and their typewriter keys were well out reach of the new teenage bitter-gargler on the scene.

My first breakthrough came with my first front page by-line, but that was not without its own problems.

TV panellist Lady Isobel Barnett had become something of an eccentric recluse, and filled in her spare time with a spot of shop-lifting. When the bizzies closed in, she decided to end her days with an overdose in the bath, and I was on my own in the newsroom when the PA (Press Association) news tape began its familiar chatter.

Don Aldred, the pipe-smoking news editor, read the information and announced that this would do for the front page lead on the lunchtime edition. I was to knock it into a story and that would be my first major outing in the journalistic world.

The problem was that the paper was also known among less-kind readers as the 'Telegraph and Misprint', and so after I had phoned all my family and friends with the joyous news, the presses rolled with 40,000 copies announcing 'Isobel Barnett found dead in bath' with the by-line 'by Tum Humphries'. And for the next four years, everybody called me Tum.

Chapter Six
Anfield Call-Up

THE year 1981 was a memorable one at Valley Parade because the mighty Liverpool came calling in the second round of the League Cup. And City had the temerity to beat Ian Rush and all the rest of them 1-0 in the home leg.

The city partied for three successive nights in an 'end of war' party atmosphere but, ahead of the second leg at Anfield, the Telegraph had injury worries of their own after 'Mr Bradford City' David Markham went down with flu and was unable to go over to Merseyside and do the preview pieces.

Don asked for a volunteer to go over with a photographer, and I nearly knocked the pipe out of his mouth as my arm shot up.

We got to Melwood and took pictures of the Liverpool boys in training and this lovely old grandad of a Geordie made a right fuss of us in his cardigan and his slippers. Bob Paisley then invited us to Anfield to take pictures of the away dressing room, before he led us along to the tunnel.

"You have to touch this sign, because all the players do," he said, pointing to 'This Is Anfield' and the red liver bird above the tunnel entrance, and then it was down the narrow steps. At the bottom there was a plain old garden shed door, and then there were two steps up and you were on the green sward of Anfield itself.

I had read countless books written by goalkeepers about playing in front of the Kop for the first time, about this great sea of humanity that went back for ever and ever. But, from the mouth of the tunnel at pitch-side, both ends looked the same.

"Which is the Kop?" I asked my new best mate, Bob. He looked at me, turned on his heel, and walked up the stairs. Interview over. You don't fuck with Bob Paisley and the Kop.

Chapter Seven
Back Home

BEFORE I entered the world of journalism, I had rubbed shoulders with sporting gods on home soil at Headingley when Geoff Boycott scored his 100th century in an Ashes match against Australia. The only problem was that me and my three fellow truants were supposed to be at school.

Actually that wasn't the only problem. We had also painted a sign on a bed sheet which stated that Boycott was a Yorkshire legend and that if there was any justice in the world (and should any ill fortune befall Queen Elizabeth who admittedly appeared to be in the rudest of health) then he should be king of England.

Another problem was that we hadn't considered the possibility of this bed sheet appearing on the night-time TV highlights, fluttering proudly and vigorously in the wind above the heads of four young boys who should have been in double physics at that precise moment.

Still, it was a glorious afternoon, and the subsequent four hours of detention did nothing to diminish my love of the sport.

But, back in the world of high-flying journalism, our well-intentioned idiot was to receive another jolt in his life when he was to meet the woman of his dreams.

We were sent on three-month block release courses to Darlington Technical College to study journalism and, while I travelled up from Bradford, a stunning young lady called Maria Conn journeyed up from the Midlands for her spot at the far from hallowed seat of learning.

Being a teacher's pet sort, her seat was at the front of the class, and it was there that she was perched when I walked into the classroom on the inaugural day and set eyes on her for the first time. "Oh, my God, I'm going to marry you," I said, but not out loud obviously. But if you saw her, you would say the same thing.

It took about four years and a hell of a lot of chloroform to bring her around to my way of thinking.

The first problem was how to fix up a date. I got my typewriter and hid it under a pile of clothes at the bottom of the wardrobe in my digs, and then went back to college and asked Maria if it would be possible to call round to her place that evening and borrow her typewriter because I had left mine at home in the rush to travel up to the even more frozen parts of the north of the country.

She kindly agreed, so I stuck my guitar and a bottle of wine under the car seat and set off to our first date in my finest white cheesecloth shirt and jeans ensemble (it was 1980, cut us some slack here). Anyway, before I got to grips with her typewriter, I suggested that we had a couple of drinks at the jazz club at Darlington Tech to begin the evening with a swing.

At this point, I really should introduce you to Penny, who was the fly in the ointment at this moment – or should more accurately and fairly be described as my fiancee.

We had met on my previous visit to Darlington 12 months earlier, on the initial three-month block release, and we had ended up living together down in Bradford through an unfortunate set of circumstances.

She was lovely to look at and a bubbly character, and she was quite keen early on to go on the pill so that we could have sex, which is always a clincher in anyone's book in my opinion.

She was also adopted, which is where the heart strings got confused and led to us overthinking things, because all of a sudden my emotions got strung out and I felt that we were destined to save each other. Everything totally misted over the fact that she was a loony that could have easily given my poor sainted mother a run for her money.

The latter became ever more apparent after we moved in together down in Bradford following a rapid engagement, and by the time I returned to Darlington for my second stint of learning the journalistic mysteries of law and public administration, I already felt over-qualified in the mysteries of women.

Fast forward to the jazz club, and who should walk in while Maria and I were checking out each other's tonsils, but the lovely Penny.

The latter reacted like a fly who disturbed the ointment and was far from gruntled, and I said to Maria: "Oh, hang on. There's just something that I've got to sort out." Remember that line.

Taking Penny gently by the arm, I led her outside the establishment, whereupon she surprisingly threw herself into a bush and started thrashing around angrily while I tried quickly to get out the lines that I had been rehearsing in my head for the last three months.

"I know you're angry, but things have not been working out well for a while now, and I think that you should really go back and live with your mum while we sort things out," I tried to reason. She replied with several things, the most coherent of which seemed to be: "Bastard!"

(I thought that was quite hurtful, given the circumstances that we both found ourselves in, but on rapid reflection I did not feel that this was perhaps the right time to pursue the matter).

Anyway, she agreed for me to drive her home to her mother's, and all seemed to be going relatively swimmingly until the point where she decided to get out of the car again while we were travelling at 30 mph.

I slammed the brakes on and she bounced a couple of times before rolling to a halt, and I jumped out of the car and ran around to where she lying, looking quite dazed and a little cut and bruised.

It was the wrong time to feel that way, but your heart never gives a damn about these things, and I couldn't help but love her and think about all the people that had let her down up to that point in her life. Right now, I was probably the worst one of the lot.

I scooped her up in my arms, placed her back in the passenger seat, and drove on to her mum's house. Knocking on the door, I passed her over and said: "Would you please look after her cos she's nuts," and then did the time-honoured thing by running away.

On getting back to the aforementioned jazz club, I walked in. Now, dear reader, put yourself in Maria's place in front of your gin and grapefruit (again, don't judge, because she drank shit but still tasted sweet) and picture the scene from her point of view.

The bloke that you're on your first date with has just reappeared, with his previously all-white ensemble now smeared with a surfeit of blood, and the last thing that he has said to you is: "Oh, hang on. There's just something that I've got to sort out."

Would you even consider a second date with him? Much less go on to enjoy a 36-year-marriage and share two glorious children and two breath-taking grand-daughters? And you thought my mother was nuts.

Chapter Eight
Career

SO, with Penny now fully qualified to compare notes with my mother about the more giving wallpaper world, and the rest of life settling down to whatever counts for normality in our lives, me and Maria got on with our everyday existences while conducting a courtship based on occasional stolen weekends together while living the best part of 100 miles apart.

I carried on trying to forge a career in journalism at the Telegraph and Argus, while Maria carried on on an increasingly upward path at her paper in the Midlands where she went from cub reporter to deputy news editor, to news editor in a one-newspaper career that was to eventually give her a permanent place in the history of our much-maligned (by the locals) and equally much-loved (by visitors) town of Monkstone.

My only progress of any note was from John Smith's to Guinness at lunchtimes, because I'd heard that it still gave you the necessary goodness ingredients in case you didn't eat that well.

I knew that I couldn't be an actual alcoholic because I didn't touch vodka at all, and I had read footballer Jimmy Greaves's autobiography all about that stuff twice.

Anyway I couldn't be an alcoholic because I didn't get hangovers. Although the fact that I never actually sobered up long enough over 40 years to get hangovers may have prevented me from them, on reflection.

But, despite getting more and more column inches on the sports pages from writing on the non-League exploits of Thackley, Guiseley and Farsley Celtic, my heart was no longer in it, and the entire reason for my being was living 100 miles away in the Midlands.

So, I decided to follow my heart. I gave up my job as a journalist and took any work that I could find further down south.

That job turned out to be the commercial manager of Grantham Town Football Club. In fact, it wasn't really a job as such. Because I didn't get paid.

I was on 5% commission of any money that I raised for the club and, after three months when I hadn't raised any money at all (which is always looked upon as a demerit mark for a commercial manager), I resigned 30 minutes before an emergency board meeting was organised to relieve me of my duties. I felt that the resignation would look better on my CV.

But at least I was closer to Maria. But that didn't seem to improve the bond between us, and in fact she seemed to prefer it for some reason when we had that 90-mile buffer between us that separated Bradford and Monkstone and a totally in love up to the gills boy and a beautiful young woman that could have her pick of the countryside.

Chapter Nine
A Good Face for Radio

AFTER what I learned about the job by not doing it properly at Grantham Town, I fared a little better in my next job as commercial manager at Worksop Town, where I put into action the right way about doing things in terms of raising money, although things did not get off to the best of starts.

I got a four-point booking and a £25 fine from simply sitting in the stand for our Northern Premier League match at Lancaster City.

We went up on the coach on one of those glorious North Western afternoons of mists and mellow fruitfulness that encapsulate autumnal afternoons in Britain and make you wonder why people ever want to emigrate. Until you realise that you are sat in an old wooden stand and can't actually feel your fingers any more through your thermal gloves.

And then a player was dying on the pitch. Our trainer ran on without getting permission from the referee because he realised that, following a clash of heads during an aerial challenge, one of the Worksop Town players had swallowed his tongue.

He managed to release the player's tongue and got him breathing again, and then noticed that the match official was standing over him and brandishing a yellow card.

"Name?" asked the official, officiously. "Humphries!" yelled our trainer in his face. I was the only Humphries officially registered at the club, and so the four disciplinary points and the £25 fine were heading my way until the club secretary intervened and sorted out the misunderstanding to the satisfaction of all parties concerned.

Not a great start, but the phone in the board room was red hot as our young commercial manager provided a dual benefit for the club by downing pint after pint of lager from the club bar during the course of the day while phoning companies all over Worksop, Rotherham and Doncaster and the surrounding areas and raking in money like there was no tomorrow.

But while Worksop Town Football Club was doing very nicely thank you, the Tigers' chairman Jack Isherwood was not a happy bunny when he saw the size of his phone bill at the end of each month (even though the size of the bar income would have more than evened things out).

He decided that his benevolence towards the club would know no bounds, and that he would solve the problem by getting the young commercial manager to come and set up his stall in the back of his fish and chip shop on the corner of the Sandy Lane ground. And so it was there, next to the huge mushy peas vat, that my subsequent dealings in the vast world of South Yorkshire and North Nottinghamshire finance were made.

It was when I had just completed a shirt sponsorship deal worth a tidy sum, and replaced the phone in its cradle, only to witness the back of my hand covered in mushy peas, that I decided the time was nigh to move on.

The next port of call was to my beloved Leeds United, which should have been far more glamorous than it actually was.

The team was in the process of being relegated over a long and depressing season under the management of former goal-scoring hero Allan Clarke, and the depressive atmosphere clung to the stands, the people, and the very fabric of the place whose protagonists used to adorn my bedroom walls as a child. It was horrible.

On the first day that I was there, I reversed into Allan Clarke's car in the car park and I was told off for whistling in the corridor by the crisply-suited shiny-shoed commercial manager.

The other downside was that I was back in West Yorkshire and was once again 100 miles away from the person that my whole world revolved around.

The upside was that I got a job on a radio station, although it was ironically indirectly because of Leeds United that I got sacked. Which was a shame, because I had a good face for radio.

The game in question that I was sent to report on for Pennine Radio was Leicester City versus Leeds United at Filbert Street.

The best thing about my job as a football journalist was coming over the brow of a hill and seeing the ground before you, with the floodlights reaching proudly for the sky yet somehow arching protectively over the ground nestling below.

It's a buzz that, for me, could only be replicated by marching across the tarmac at an airfield with a helmet under your arm about to climb into a fighter aircraft as a Top Gun pilot – and I still struggle to see the homosexual connotations in that particular film (even though my other favourite films are Notting Hill and Mamma Mia. Whatever. Shut up).

Anyway. I was sent there with a briefcase and a brief. Two-minute preview; 22 minutes score-line update; half-time, etc. You put the briefcase on the press bench, open it up, and there is a plug, a microphone which pops up with a red button next to it, and headphones.

When you put the headphones on, there is the producer through the right can (invariably camp) and the radio station live through the left can, and when you hit the red button, you are live.

The crucial bit in this story is that when you hit the red button again, the microphone is dead. Remember that, dear reader. Should you forget that, then you too could be sacked during the live radio coverage of a football match.

So after 22 minutes of a reasonably even contest, with neither side looking remotely likely to trouble the scorers, the following sequence of events took place:-

Producer (right can): "Okay, TJ darling, we're ready to have you in three, two, one…

Radio show (left can): "And now we can go over to Filbert Street, where our reporter at the First Division match is Tim Humphries."

Producer (right can): "Go, TJ love!"

Me, concluding the piece: "… And so, the score here from Filbert Street is still … Leicester City 0… Leeds United 0."

Producer (right can): "Super, TJ darling. See you at half-time, sugar tits."

Radio show (left can): "And now we can go over to Odsal, where our reporter at Bradford Northern versus Featherstone Rovers is…"

At that moment, Frank Worthington collects the ball in the centre circle for Leeds and spots the Leicester City goalkeeper loitering just outside his six-yard box. As only Frank Worthington (who holds the record for sexual intercourse before the kick-off of a football match; 15 minutes before a match at Anfield in the Liverpool boot room) would, he cracks a shot from the halfway line that grazes the crossbar with the City 'keeper tumbling into the back of his net in a pile of dust, and I shout the same thing that 24,000 other people shouted in unison.

"Fucking hell!!!"

The following sequence of events took place:-

Producer (right can): "TJ, hit your button, darling!!! Hit your button!!!"

Me: got sacked.

Chapter Ten
Maria's Mum

JUST before New Year in 1984, Maria bought a delightful cottage in Monkstone on a little leafy-covered hidden away muse. It was as mystical and romantic and spider-infested as it sounds. She was still as fit as a butcher's dog (that means very good looking in Yorkshire). She still is. It is worth remembering this when she spends her every waking hour crying.

It was bought with money that she had been left by her aunty. It was on the cusp of New Year that her mum was diagnosed with breast cancer and Maria was afraid that it was the end, so she asked to me to travel down to be with her so that I could hold her while she cried.

I had also had a stroke of luck on the job front and had collared the deputy sports editor's job on the Barnsley Chronicle as the number two to the great Keith Lodge, childhood friend of the legendary cricket umpire Dickie Bird who was to go on to bug us every Thursday morning if he wasn't standing somewhere in the world at a cricket match.

He'd sit on the edge of the sports desk and drink tea and talk bollocks while we flew around on press day trying to get the paper to bed.

I later gave him cause to write a letter to the MCC at Lord's explaining that he actually had no intention of retiring from umpiring after I had revealed the fact to the world exclusively on the back page of the Barnsley Chronicle while Keith was on holiday in South Wales (having entrusted his deputy not to mess things up while he was enjoying a well-earned break).

Keith had a holiday cottage in Tenby where he used to cherish his two week chill every year, leaving me with the cheery message: "Any problems – don't phone me."

He couldn't have anticipated the shock waves that this story would send across the sporting world, with the news that cricket's most famous ever man in a white cap would be calling it a day.

In my flimsy defence, I was panicking. I didn't really know how to do page lay-outs and do sub-editing, and I was making it up by ear most of the time, and getting away with it as usual.

But the deadline was getting closer and closer and the clock was ticking along in a cartoon manner while I still had a big hole on the back page where that week's lead story should be. In walked Dickie.

"It's my 94th international cricket match as an umpire at the next week, mate," he mused, as he sipped from his steaming polystyrene cup.

"Oh yeah, Dickie," I said, ignoring him while in full panic attack mode, and nervously contemplating both the end of my career and my finger nails.

"Who would have thought that me, Harold Bird, would get to that sort of number of matches at the very top level out in the middle?"

"Yeah, Dickie. Amazing, mate." Suddenly it clicked. I clutched my last remaining straw and reached for my dictaphone surreptitiously.

"Have you ever thought about calling it a day at 100, Dickie? You know, finishing on a nice, round figure," asked the devious bastard who should have been wearing one of those see-through medicine-coloured visors with his sleeves rolled up and a half-smoked cheroot behind his ear.

I can see me asking the question as clear as a bell right now as I sit hunched over this keyboard, making at the time – as I so clearly was – no less than a pact with the devil.

"Why, now you mention it, that would seem to be perfect, wouldn't it," replied my victim, twitching slightly as he allowed himself to be ensnared into my clutches. Gotcha, Dickie Bird!

ONE HUNDRED AND OUT! DICKIE TO QUIT!

The 72-point banner headline, with a correctly spelt 'by TIM HUMPHRIES', blared out of the back pages of the Barnsley Chronicle on Friday morning, and by lunchtime the local parasites had wired the copy down to the London papers and across the world to make their sixty pieces of silver as Dickie's carcass swung from a tree.

He had to write a cringing letter to Lord's, bless him, saying that he had been stitched up by a young wet-behind-the-ears-reporter who knew no better.

It is a credit to the wonderful, loving and generous characters of Keith Lodge and Dickie Bird that they still talked to me to the last day that I met them.

And I am truly blessed to count them among the treasured friends that I have been privileged to meet over the years (That's enough now – KL.)

So anyway, Maria said I could stay there at her cottage until I found a house in Barnsley. I never looked.

Chapter Eleven
Kondios

THERE'S a great man called Jim Moran, who gave me the best piece of advice that I have ever been given. He was very rare – a photographer who was also a nice bloke. They're normally a pain in the arse.

I worked with him in Sheffield at a wonderfully-named newspaper called 'The North Sheffield Shopper'. You will know his work. Remember the picture of the half of the cockpit of the 747 in the field near Lockerbie after the mid-air bomb attack – Jim took that.

I chose him as our wedding photographer because I loved working with him, and I loved the quality of his work, but I didn't really know the quality of the man until he spoke to me on the night before the wedding.

He said: "Do yourself a favour tomorrow, mate. Don't have a drink until you get to the honeymoon hotel down in London, and then you will be able to remember every single minute of what will be the best day of your entire life."

If you name me any single minute of our wedding day, I will be able to recall what happened with forensic accuracy at that exact time. From the moment that I walked into that classroom in Darlington to that day, that had been my goal.

To marry the most wonderful girl in the world, and the most beautiful human being – inside and out – that I have ever seen or met in my life. We took a video of the wedding, which is obsolete these days. I don't need it. The memories will last for ever.

The honeymoon was miraculous because Maria organised it all herself – it wasn't available on a package holiday deal. We went to a little Greek island called Kondios, which no-one had heard of, and which had no hotels or airports.

You got a flight to Athens and then a two-hour ferry ride, and then we were there for three weeks. Apart from the obvious, the highlights (which lasted a hell of a lot longer) were living in a single room above a taverna, fresh fish every day, watching Boris Becker win the Men's Wimbledon tennis title as a 17-year-old kid, and watching Live Aid on the ferry back to Athens surrounded by the local families and their goats.

Absolute heaven. It was so good that we went back for our Silver Wedding Anniversary. Nothing had changed except that they had built a hotel and we had got a bit wider. And the arguments went on a bit longer.

Chapter Twelve
Billem

WE WERE delighted when Maria got pregnant with our first child, and we decided to call him Billy if it was a boy or Emma if it was a girl. We called it Billem when we had a miscarriage.

I've always got on with God. I didn't really have a choice, because He was with me from the start, but I like to think that, like Glenn Hoddle, I would have found Him in the end. I've always thought that that must have been one hell of a pass, even by Glenn's standards.

But I was raised by my parents as a Catholic and, in the time-honoured phrase, they were pretty devout. No swearing was allowed in our house and no suggestion of anything untoward was allowed.

My dad was like a male Mary Whitehouse. When anything slightly risqué came on the television, he would stand in front of it and studiously wind the clock up – even though I'm pretty sure it ran on batteries.

When Maria came to our house for the first time, we followed up the traditional celebratory meal of meat and roast protestants – sorry, potatoes – by gathering round the television and watching "It Ain't Half Hot, Mum", not because it was a family favourite (far too risqué) but because it was on at the time, and everyone was too nervous to change the channel.

During the show there was an explosion, and Willie lost his necklace with his name on it. When he exclaimed: "I have lost my Willie!", Maria gave out a huge belly laugh, and you could have cut the air with a cassock.

There was a similar atmosphere on another occasion when she described something as 'crap' and I would willingly have swopped the moment for having my toenails removed with a blunt stick.

We also had to go to Mass on the evening of the first Friday of every month, but I never thought to ask the question: "What the fuck is this all about?" You live to regret chances missed, I guess.

But I served on the altar after making my First Holy Communion – when I remember the jelly rather than the spiritually uplifting occasion – and I actively considered becoming a priest until the age of 16 when I discovered beer and women. Unfortunately I read 'Thornbirds' far too late.

So God and I got on just fine, and we never really had cross words until me and Maria had our miscarriage. Then God and I fell out big style.

I asked Him what the hell that was all about. Because we weren't bad people who did bad things. So why would He deny us the chance to give a baby all the love in the world – especially in my family that had never had the opportunity to have a baby arrive in it in the normal way that the rest of the world just takes for granted.

As they would say in the best Church of England homes, I was right royally fucked off with God and He was told about it in no uncertain terms. In fact I told Him that I wasn't going to go to Mass any more.

Which, if you think about it, is actually a form of praying. So the big man has got all the bases covered. Cunning bastard. You've got to kind of admire Him for that.

By the way, when I told my parish priest at Monkstone in later years that I had once considered a life in the priesthood, he smiled at me and said: "You would have made a remarkable priest, TJ, but it is a fairly safe bet that after every one of your sermons, you could have expected a call from the bishop."

Chapter Thirteen
Abigail Jane

SO the days at the cottage came to an end. We knew that the time was up when the stairs collapsed, leaving me at the top of them laughing hysterically, but the place always had the lingering air of miscarriage hanging over it in the end.

We set our sights on a new home, and Maria's mum had a dream where she saw us living happily in that house. And, let's face it, she is the closest thing that I've ever met to a witch, so it was sort of written in the stars.

Our new house, which we were to live in for the next 32 years (and which our eldest daughter, her husband and their two daughters live in now, which is a wonderful, cosy feeling) was a magnificent family home and was superbly well predicted by my mother-in-law, the witch.

It had an Anderson air raid shelter at the bottom of the garden, as it was built at the time of the Second World War, and the shelter would have made a great drinking den if it wasn't for the spiders that had already established their own base down there and had the attitude of seriously pissed off Hell's Angels.

And very quickly, Maria was pregnant again, though I was under strict instruction not to mention anything to anybody just in case God decided to be a pain in the arse again about it.

But I think it must have been obvious to everyone when I went off to report on a game in Monkstone on a Sunday afternoon and won the raffle at a football match for the first time ever.

I walked around with a massive teddy bear zipped inside my jacket, and a smile the size of the Partick Thistle mascot on my face. Nice God was with me that day.

When Abbi was born I thought it was going to be the best day of my life. Instead it appeared to be destined to be the worst. It turned out that I was wrong on that score as well.

Maria was in labour in hospital for 28 hours, and it was only the gas and air that kept me going. This may be where I lose the sympathy of all the women that have been rooting for me so far, but screw you, ladies.

We men have a major part to play in this as well. We have all the worry of seeing the people we love in absolute agony for all that period of time with nothing at all that we can do about, while taking all the abuse under the sun about how useless that we are, and that without us you wouldn't be in this state at all, and you seem to have forgotten that it was you who said oh go on then just one more drink what harm can it do and…

It was shit.

And then it was a girl.

As I looked over the blood and gore and winked and said: "Just one more stitch, cheers pal," I saw that I was not going to be able to take my boy to the football. And I wasn't happy. And when she started breast feeding…! But, after about three months, she became my best mate.

She will hate me for writing this down on a page for so many others to peruse over, but I love you, Abbi (she will say she hates it, but there will be a tear rolling down her face because she takes after her mother).

Abbi is another remarkable woman, who is stronger than she will ever know (I felt Anna flinch with jealousy just then) and I am so proud of how you have put up with all you have done over the years.

Especially now when your best friend has gone and our family will never be the same again, no matter how we try. But, God knows, we will.

And we will try, and there will be good times, but Anna will always be just tantalisingly out of reach, no matter how we stretch out for her with our hands and our hearts.

And her laughter – her gorgeous, infectious, rib-tickling laughter – will always be a wonderful memory, playing teasingly on the air around and just above our heads.

Chapter Fourteen
Anna Louise

WE TRIED so very hard to make a friend for Abbi to play with. In the end, I sank down on my knees in the spare room after we had made love one more time, and I prayed harder than I've prayed before in my life so that we could have another baby. And along came Anna.

She was gorgeous. I'm not just saying it as her dad. Everyone said it. Because she was. Is. I don't know how you say it of someone who is dead but who is still alongside you every time you breath out. Or laugh. Or cry. Or argue. Or tell God that he is a FIRST CLASS CUNT.

When Anna was born, I just looked at her and said: "Oh, my God. I love you." I didn't care that she was a girl. I just loved her, body and soul. She was a gift from God, and she reminded me of that every time that we argued.

"You prayed for me!" she would shout, and I always countered her argument with: "Be careful of what you pray for!"

Be careful of what you pray for. If God gives you something that is truly sent from heaven – as Anna was – then I suppose that He has every right to take it back when He wants. Fair does.

When I was drinking heavily after her death, I argued with God all the time. Now, 164 days since my last drop at the time of writing, we discuss things passionately, but I am getting to see His point more and more and I think that our friendship is deepening because I am getting to understand His mysterious ways a little better.

I am also getting a little bit older, and gaining wisdom through my grandchildren. And gaining awareness through my body and its increasing various creaks that it might not be long before I am going to meet God face to face.

It might be a good time for us to be on speaking terms, rather than me calling Him a cunt. Although, having said that, I bet they have better parties in Hell.

Chapter Fifteen
Maria Joins the Mafia

MARIA has always gone to church with me, but she had never joined in. She has always gone along and sat there and sang along with the hymns and made up the words to the prayers to go along with the rest of the crowd.

My favourite line about growing up in the Catholic Church is from my all-time favourite comedian Billy Connolly who said that when he was dragged up in the faith he was convinced that there is a teddy in heaven called Gladly who had a squint, because they kept singing the hymn: 'Gladly the cross I'd bear.'

Anyhoo, the kids eventually got to that age where they started playing up and got used to the effects of the sharp shock of the electric cattle prod, so we had to try a different tactic.

We went to see my mum and dad up in Bradford for the weekend and went to Mass at St Clare's on Sunday morning where I had first learned that serving on the altar is a good place to ogle girls from (little knowing that they were ogling you from down among the cheap pews. Or so we liked to muse amid the altar wine bottles afterwards when the priest had buggered off).

Then, right at the start of Mass, this bloke stood up with a book and walked to a room at the side of the altar, and all the little kids followed him like the Pied Piper or some holy Jim'll Fix It Club, and Maria said to herself: 'I'll have some of that.'

So she started the children's liturgy club at our church in Monkstone, where the kids go off and learn about Jesus by colouring in pictures or reading stories about The Management, while the adults do all the boring stuff about how much money the church needs off you in the collection and about how thou shalt not wank and do grown up gear until the kids join up with them after the boring sermon about the same stuff and we all fuck off to the pub. Amen.

But she didn't actually know what she should be teaching them, so she started going to Faith Talks on a Sunday afternoon from 4–5pm to learn more about Catholic life and stuff.

Then one Sunday afternoon, she came home and said: "Open a bottle of wine; I've got something to say,"

I thought, *what the fucking hell have I done now? I can't think of anything.*

And she said: "I have decided that I want to become a Catholic."

And I was gobsmacked. I had been in the Catholic faith all those 39 years and had never known the true meaning of the Holy Spirit; never experienced what I can only describe as the heroin rush through your veins of the Holy Spirit.

It courses through your body until you want to shout at the top of your lungs with all the glory that the Lord has bestowed upon your home and your family. I can recommend it.

I just said: "You keep listening to Him, love, and I will follow wherever He decides to lead you." I've got the tingle now just relating this story to you, and the tears are on the brinks of my eyelids.

I don't know, but I bet it is ten times better than heroin.

And she said: "Something inside me is telling me that I have got to go to Rome." And I said: "I think we better throw that cheese out, love."

Now Maria likes to plan family holidays 12 months in advance, because she just likes the planning. When we get wherever we are going, she wants to go home because she is homesick.

But this conversation took place on a Sunday night, and on Thursday morning we are touching down at Leonardo Da Vinci Airport (yeah, right, just you think about putting this book down now and going to bed, mate).

And I'm thinking: "Okay, God. You've fucking done it this time. Let's go."

She who must be obeyed (because she's got really cracking tits) said: "I want to go along to St Peter's to the 10 o'clock Mass, and then go down and get my first blessing…"

(In the Catholic Church, you can go down to communion and get the bread and wine providing you are a Catholic. If you are not, or if you have collected four bookings under the disciplinary procedures or have got divorced, then you can go down for a blessing, which involves crossing your arms across your chest and the priest then makes the sign of the cross in front of you)

"… and then go outside and have an audience with the Pope in St Peter's Square."

"Okay, love, if you want to do things by half, that's fair enough."

So on the Friday, we went to St Peter's to have a recce, and it was crap. The Holy Spirit wasn't in and St Peter had gone fishing for the day. It was just full of tourists following the green umbrellas, and I said to her: "You're not wasting an occasion like your first blessing here. Come on, let's go."

After breakfast the following morning, we went for a walk around the red light area near our hotel at the back of the station (I know how to treat a girl, but you can take a man out of Yorkshire…) and we popped into Santa Maria Maggiore, which is one of the five basillicas (little cathedrals) in Rome.

The place was deserted, and as we walked down the aisle a shaft of sunlight suddenly poured down directly on us, causing us to jump backwards in surprise. I gasped and said: "Okay, God, back off. You've made your point. We'll come here tomorrow."

The following day at 10 o'clock Mass, Maria walked nervously down the aisle to receive her first blessing, and promptly burst into tears and ran out of the church. I took communion and followed her out and put my arms round her.

She said: "Sod this. Let's go to the pub." I laughed and kissed her and said: "I think you're a Catholic already."

At the Easter Vigil that followed back in Monkstone she joined the Mob.

Chapter Sixteen
Death's Door

THE following story is true, and only human emotions have been altered to respect the daughter of witchcraft.

We were due to go on the Eurostar to Paris the following day as part of my 48th birthday celebrations, and I had prepared in my usual way with eight pints and 40 cigarettes at lunchtime, because I didn't think that it was right to upset my usual routine with a big day coming up.

I was in the front room watching a nature programme on BBC2, and Maria and the girls were watching Emmerdale in the back room. Suddenly I felt an attack of indigestion across my chest, and I called out to Maria to complain of my predicament.

"Don't bother us. We're watching Emmerdale," called back my beloved. "If you are that bothered there is some Gaviscon in the upstairs bathroom cabinet."

(If you are reading this book as part of your research for a career in the medical field, Gaviscon is not a medication recommended for heart attacks. However, if you're studying in Newark-on-Trent, crack on).

So I tried some, and the symptoms continued, unabated.

Another complaint brought the response: "Well, the hospital's only across the road. Go there if you're worried, but stop bothering us."

I wasn't able to get any more comfortable, no matter how much I plumped up the cushions, so I thought that it would be worth nipping over the road just to justify my council tax or however these things work.

I went up to the counter at the Accident and Emergency unit and said: "I'm awfully sorry to bother you, but I feel really strange. I don't want to cause a fuss, but I feel as though I have swallowed a zimmer frame."

Instead of ushering me into a waiting room, giving me an aspirin, and telling me to wait there for three hours that I'd never get back (or two whole Notts County matches, for Christ's sake) I was rushed into a side ward and had my shirt ripped open as they started sticking electrodes all over my chest.

I said: "Hey, I said I didn't want to cause a fuss," and the nurse said: "Shut up, sir. You're having a heart attack."

After things calmed down a bit, a doctor said to me: "Is there anyone that we can call?"

I said: "My wife is just over the road," and gave them our phone number.

Maria came in in floods of tears, and the doctor took her arm and said: "Don't worry, madam. He is going to be okay."

And she said: "No. It's not that. The baby died on Emmerdale."

I was put on a ward in a bed right in front of the nurses' window, and it only hurt once, in what seemed as though it was the middle of the night.

51

I yelled out in pain, and the nurse said: "How bad is it, marks out of ten?"

And I said: "Well, my wife says that I have a very low pain threshold."

The nurse said: "I can't see her here right now. How bad is it, marks out of ten?"

I said: "Eight and a half." And she jabbed a syringe of morphine into an important vein and I went to sleep watching a lovely mural on the wall, which wasn't there in the morning. I can recommend morphine. It's on a par with the Holy Spirit.

It took me a week to realise that I was on the intensive care ward, although the tombstone at the bottom of the bed should have been a bit of a clue. As should the fact that people kept dying on a regular basis.

But the survivors got together quite a good little club, and breakfast was the topic that gave us all a common theme during the rest of the day, so we used to gather at the foot of someone's bed in our dressing gowns and compare notes.

When someone had died during the night, they used to pull the curtains round the bed, until the vultures popped in from the Disney cartoons with their stretchers and carted them off.

"Did you have the toast this morning?"

"Yeah. Lovely, wasn't it? With the way that butter just melted off the end."

"Brown bread?"

"Shhhh," someone would whisper, gesturing towards some closed curtains…

At the end of the week, the plum in the gob specialist came on his rounds to see me and said: "If there's no more pain, you can go home tomorrow morning, my good man."

I said: "Thank you very much. It has actually only hurt the once since I came in here, to be honest. But, you lot started it – how bad was it – the heart attack? Marks out of ten?"

"Oh," he said, grinning and clapping me fondly on the shoulder, "I think you'll find that it was a good eight and a half, sir."

Chapter Seventeen
Mental Health

MENTAL health is something that has always had a special home in my family, regrettably. My mum obviously had her problems and she eventually passed away in a home where she was given special care and attention and people ate their paper hats at Christmas.

People often ask me where I get my sense of humour from, and I tell them about the morning that my dad broke the news to me when my mum died.

The phone went at 6.30am in Monkstone and I answered it bleary eyed with a half asleep: "Hello."

"Your mother passed away half an hour ago," croaked the barely recognisable voice of a man that I loved like no other on the planet.

"You're joking!" I shouted, now fully wide awake and slipping seamlessly into full panic mode.

"No, Timothy. If I was joking, I would have said: 'Knock, Knock,'" said dad, and we both laughed out loud.

Anna and I regularly laughed out loud over our joint mental illnesses, although hers were a lot worse than mine, because I am still here, and she's in a covered box in Maria's room.

If I am asked to repeat that paragraph on television as part of a means of plugging this book, then I will not be able to hold back the tears. As I cannot now.

So yeah, this shit's been around for the best part of 60 years, plaguing the family.

When I was a kid, I was constantly aware of it and used to be taken to visit my mum when she was at the forbidding mental institution at Menston near Ilkley, though I'm not sure how good an idea that was for the growing awareness of a developing three-year-old. If you were teetering on the edge, that building would give you the nudge.

Years later, the former Rugby League commentator Eddie Waring was apparently a lodger at the same gaff, and who would have ever thought that he was nuts?

But my own mental health issues were alive and kicking as a young kid – fear of being kidnapped, and a fear that anything that happened on the news that day was going to happen to me at some stage later in the week. Though earthquakes were a rarity in downtown Fagley, even in the cheap seats of Eccleshill.

As I got older, I discovered that alcohol could take some of the edges off my fears and, although I escaped the worst of its clutches for as long as possible, it did get to a stage where I used to take a swig out of the numerous bottles on the sideboard before stepping out into the world beyond the front door, and I used to light the unsmoked stubs in the stacked unemptied ashtrays that were always littered around on the arms of chairs.

After the heart attack, I stopped smoking, from 40-a-day-plus to zilch overnight, and I also stopped drinking until Maria told me that I was boring and she wanted her husband back to make her laugh again.

Fast forward to the last few years, and on a day off, I would think nothing of pursuing the following itinerary:-

9:15 am-ish: Shower, shave and clean my teeth;

9:40 am: Good book, comfy chair in the garden room, couple of cans of Dark Fruit and a bottle of Cava;

11:30 am: Take book to the pub; three pints of Dark Fruit and three double whisky chasers;

3 pm: Home, lunch (I'm not an animal); sleep on the bed;

5 pm: Take book to the pub; three pints of Dark Fruit and three double whisky chasers;

8 pm: Bottle of red wine;

10 pm: Bed.

Tomorrow: Rinse and repeat.

And that was primarily to feel better about life and to cope with sporadic panic attacks and the more or less constant anxiety.

Chapter Eighteen
Anna Louise

ME and Anna fought like cat and dog, but we basically were very good drinking buddies.

You would think that, given my start in life, where I began without a family, I would have thrown myself into family life and relished every minute of being in a tight-knit bosom of a home.

I've no doubt that psychiatrists will have the answer why, but I preferred to be a loner with a book and a beer in a cosy alcove somewhere while Maria and the girls went off and played somewhere together.

The newspaper came first; the priority was getting the pages to bed, and then celebrating the achievement, and numbing the thought of more work to come the following day before crashing out into an exhausted sleep and snoring for England.

So I was a crap dad, because I was so consumed by anxiety, and by the need to get my work done, and then the need to go out and celebrate having got through the day, and then the need to kill the pain at the thought of having to do it all again tomorrow, so all I wanted to do was get drunk to feel better and then make love to my beautiful wife.

Maria was understandably not always so keen to make love to this guy who was getting fatter by the day, with more and more extreme mood swings, but sometimes she was as drunk as me, so that worked out just fine.

By the time I was a granddad, I was a different person. I gave up drinking ten days before Jenny was born, because I wanted to have a clear head to welcome her into the world and not to just sit there and hold her in my arms and cry because I thought it was wonderful because I was full up to the brim with alcohol.

So, I was able to live a normal grandad life. And I had also by that stage packed up the stressful side of jobs in the main, although my time as communications officer with Monkstone Football Club was a cause of anger in its own way when I constantly had to beg the chairman for the pittance that he paid me each month.

I was offered £350 a month to write the programmes for the matches, write the match reports for the local newspaper and Monkstone FM, where I did a voluntary assistant producer's role on a sports show for four nights a week for five years for an arsehole called George Hammond.

I thought George and I were very close, but he never let me know when he finished the show and decided to go off with his mate – our Thursday night boy – and do the programme on-line. I found about that when he thanked all the guests over the last five years on Facebook.

More of a mark of the man was that he never sent me a message of condolence when Anna hanged herself, and even the football club secretary Les Stannard – the self-styled LS who was a fellow dim-witted arsehole-in-crime who shares a brain cell with Hammond – managed that.

I left a message on Facebook that George Hammond could go fuck himself as my way of leaving Monkstone FM, and also resigned from my position as communications officer of Monkstone Football Club after finally having enough of the chairman, whose foul body odour created as bad a stink as the bullshit promises that he filled people with about the football club.

I was told that the £350 a month would be increased if the club got promoted, or if I proved to be any good at the job. After two successive promotions, a cup win, and a Programme of the Year Award, I still had to remind him that I had not seen my £350 in my bank each month – a sum that apparently you get more than if you go on the dole.

One enlightened individual who used to be a good friend also advised me during this heightened personal mental health period that I needed 'to give my head a shake'.

Because of the chairman's incompetence, or lack of concern, Monkstone Football Club lost their ground housing and had to leave the town to go and play miles away, losing the majority of their fan base in the process, which was the most impressive thing about the whole venture.

I still love the club with all my heart, and I will wear their colours around the town long after the club has ceased to exist – and it is on borrowed time now.

But Abbi and Anna were made for one another, as me and Maria had intended in the first place. They played together non-stop and, although they had other friends, and made them very easily, they felt at most at ease together and – despite the two years and nine months between them – they were more like twins than anything else, which makes the absence all the more painful for Abbi.

Anna also loved slapstick comedy and would have made a superb stand-up comedienne herself, because her sense of timing and the surreal was exceptional. She was also exceptionally good looking and had a figure like Jessica Rabbit. And, oh boy, did she know it.

She had a string of boyfriends, some of them less objectionable than others, and Abbi once asked me if I thought that Anna just picked knobs or was it a case that we would never think that anyone was good enough for her. Then we both laughed and said, yeah, it was because they were all knobs.

She was a lot like my 'sister' Carmel, in the sense that she was left-handed, vastly intelligent and clearly far too good for this world. It was clear that God had greater plans for them in heaven.

It was when she got to university that she appeared to have found her niche in life, and she threw herself into university life to the full, reporting back to me that she had found a bar where she could get a double vodka and coke for £2.40. I told her that her grandad would be so proud of her.

But the night that she was raped by two men in her halls of residence was the start of the decline that would eventually lead to her death, and the start of ten years of severe mental health trauma that no one individual deserved to suffer. And especially not our beautiful baby.

Add that to the awful debilitating Crohn's Disease, and you have a life that became increasingly difficult to put up with, and you can't help as a journalist but to start to write it with a line like a major news story that is leading horribly towards a major disaster.

Which it was, of course, for one beautiful young woman just a few days short of her 29th birthday. Her loving, caring, family would have done anything in their power to help break her fall. But, unknown to us, Anna was planning her own suicide. The real shit. The one where you die.

Chapter Nineteen
The Day from Hell

BECAUSE of the medication that she was on due to the Crohn's Disease and the heavy duty anti-depressants, Anna was no longer able to drive, so I used to take her to and from her job that she loved as a receptionist at a factory on the town's industrial estate.

She worked with some lovely people, who turned out in force at her funeral at the crematorium.

The funeral was a week after what would have been her 29th birthday and the day after Maria's 60th birthday. Needless to say, Maria didn't celebrate her birthday in any way, so, on the rare occasions that she is actually talking to me these days, and not crying and shouting at me to leave her alone, she maintains that she is only 59. So every cloud, and all that.

So, because my entire life commitments are now as a grandad, I was free to ferry Anna to and from work. On our journeys we talked and talked about mental health problems.

I didn't know how to solve them (I do now, give up drinking) because I had been riddled with them myself for 60 years. But I knew how to laugh about them, and I knew what tickled her ribs, and every time she got out of the car at either work or at the end of the day, she was laughing.

With that wonderful luxuriant hair cascading around her face and her dimples, she had the perfect outward appearance of being the happiest girl in the world.

And, all the time, we didn't know that she was planning her own death, researching it meticulously on the Google pages.

Loving, caring Anna, who loved us all so much – well, she tolerated me, but she adored her mother and sister and her niece Jenny, who thought the world of her.

She would have never have wanted Maria to let herself into her home one morning and find the daughter that she had suffered a stroke for during labour hanging from the bannisters in front of her.

You try and sleep after seeing that again every time you close your eyes.

So we knew that Anna was in danger from herself, because she had talked about suicide before, but we didn't realise that she was just biding her time, ticking along, and waiting for the opportunity.

Or perhaps I didn't realise it. Because I wasn't allowed to be part of the gang. The inner circle. I don't know if that was because I was a boy, or if it was because I was a loner who was at his happiest in a cosy corner with a good book, his cigarettes and a few beers, and where the world had jolly well fucked off and left me well alone, thank you very much.

I had time for people when it suited me, when it was convenient. For Maria when I was horny or hungry, for the kids when it was ME that wanted to play and sod them.

All the times that I was throwing myself into piggy-back rides and making them laugh uncontrollably to the point where they would wet themselves and had tears rolling down their faces, and they would beg me to play with them all the more and make them laugh again. And be a proper dad. And I would withdraw. Back into my own shell. Is this therapy?

Or perhaps it was not me. Perhaps it was because they were all girls together, with their whispers and private things, like periods. And then the girls started growing breasts and it was: "NO! Don't come in!" behind every door.

Suicide wasn't a shock, but the day wasn't expected when it came. How could it have been?

We got a phone call from work to say that Anna was pissed and needed taking home. If Jimmy Greaves drank a bottle of vodka a day and was described as an alcoholic, it is a wonder that Anna never played for Tottenham Hotspur and England many more times than he did.

Her friend phoned us and said that the boss wasn't there, but we'd better come and get her in case anybody important came in, because Anna couldn't really stand up. So we went and got her.

From that point on, she worked from home. The last time that I saw her alive at her place, she was in a good mood, and gave me a hug which meant that she was pissed, but what the hell, she was in a good place, so that was okay.

Then, a very rapid sequence of events took place. God works in mysterious ways, my arse.

The story about my youngest daughter's last day goes like this – and it is not one that pains me to tell you about because, strangely, I can see it from her point of view.

I can sense her relief in getting away from all the shit that the world had conspired up and flung at her in ever increasing fucking bundles.

She was very drunk and very depressed, so she buggered off home, wrote a suicide note that stated "I'm sorry, I've had enough," slashed her wrists, grabbed her belt off her dressing gown and swung herself off the bannisters.

In the morning, Maria came through to the garden room where I was reading a book and drinking a coffee before setting off to get the paper without a care in the world – apart from the ever-present stupid anxiety feeling in the pit of my stomach that had no reason whatsoever to be there because life was now so wonderful.

"I'll just go check if she is okay and ready for work," said my darling wife, who still looks every bit as gorgeous as that first morning in Darlington College – although it is probably called university these days.

Less biased people may have seen an old and somewhat plump woman leaving the house (she has now lost a couple of dress sizes due to the grief and sleepless nights, and can knock out cattle from 50 yards again).

Anyway, a bit later she is back. "There's no answer. She's not answering the door. I managed to look through the lounge window, though, and there seems to be a note on the mat. I'll take a key and let myself in."

I never take my mobile phone with me when I am going to get the paper (though 'going to get the paper' is not necessary because I never take my mobile phone with me anywhere anyway, because I never had a mobile phone before I left the newspaper industry).

The phone rang all bloody day when I was at work, so I didn't want people to be able to get hold of me when I was chilling out at the pub.

I only got a mobile phone because I didn't have a computer at home, and I wanted something with a big screen to keep up to date with the football news.

But I took it with me on this occasion. I was halfway down the road on my way to the shop when my phone rang. And I just knew.

I knew what Maria was going to say before the voice that I did not recognise – but have come to know now – said: "She's dead! She's hanged herself!"

That was the moment that I wasn't scared of anything anymore.

I used to taunt myself at night time with my vivid imagination, and found it difficult to go to sleep unless I was absolutely drunk (and those sober occasions were very rare indeed over the course of 45 years) because of nightmare images of the Bradford City Fire, the Grenfell Tower Disaster, any kinds of bridges, Titanic. You name it, just dead people.

But when your worst nightmare becomes real, there is no reason to fear anything that your imagination can put together. Now I had a real dead person of my own. One that I had helped make.

So Anna saved me from fear. While saving herself from living in hell.

Good result, kid.

Chapter Twenty
And so, to the Future

THE sensible answer, obviously, was to get drunk and stay as drunk as possible.

I am an umpire at Monkstone Cricket Club, and the members – young and old – gathered round me and poured out their love for me as they showed the depth of their care and support in a tremendous way.

No-one told me how I should feel, or what I should be doing: they just sat close to me, sometimes with an arm round me, and sometimes allowed me to colour in their tattoos (just so that I could have a shoulder to crayon; sorry I just love the joke).

They were just the nicest people in the world – while Norman Clarke, my fellow umpire, put up with my drunkenness and mood swings and was just what he has always been – my second dad.

I told the groundsman, through my tears, that the club had been so kind to me in the darkest hours of my life, that when it came to my turn and I died, I wanted my ashes to be scattered at the Edwards Road ground.

He looked at me in all seriousness, and said: "That's very nice, but you're not going to bugger up the pitch; we'll put you under a tree along with Pat Davidson and Andrew McCallan's mum." I told him 'thank you' and 'that will do for me'.

Maria however imploded, and her world ended.

Now she is like really crap long-wave radio reception. Sometimes she will fade in and become quite clear, a lot like her old self and be beautiful and funny and sexy as hell without meaning to be.

At other times she will be crackly and far away like a ship that you can see through the mists; you can see that it is heading for trouble but feel powerless to do anything about it and save any of the souls that are going to be lost on it. God, I miss her then.

I don't miss Anna. She is always there. On my shoulder. Laughing at my attempts to make sense of the shit that she has left us in. But laughing with us. Not at us.

That's the problem with people that commit suicide. They're alright. They're sorted. It's over. Their pain is at an end, and they can go have a craic on a cloud and play draughts with Jesus and his mates. Good on them. It's the poor fuckers that are left down here that have to suffer. Muddling through the shit.

On Sunday July 4th, American Independence Day, it was the 45th anniversary of the day that a girl first stuck her tongue down my throat on a rock in a middle of a stream in field in the Bradford country while I fondled her breast. I hope Janet Townley is well.

Coincidentally, it was also the day that Maria told me that she was off.

"Off where?" It was seven in the morning on a sunny day which promised the glorious prospect of a gorgeous day ahead in the world outside our castle of doom.

"I've told you, I'm going with Abbi and the girls to Centre Parcs (isn't about time the French learned to spell, for le sake de Pierre). You'll have to look after yourself for the week." And then the door slammed.

"Well goodbye to you and don't forget to fuck yourself right off," I air-kissed in the direction of her cute little ass, before scratching my own. Now then, breakfast…

Stretch out your index finger and your thumb on your left hand; as far as they will go, and I had about that much whiskey left in the kitchen. Plus I had two cans of Dark Fruit in the fridge along with a bottle of Cava.

I also had a good book and a very cosy patio and a south-facing garden and a wonderful lounger facing the sun and the biggest empty gap in the pit of my stomach and a heart that was breaking and a fresh dream about killing myself that was playing over and over in my mind.

The booze did the job. I went to sleep again, which was all I wanted really. Just to block everything out and pass on some more time until I had to get drunk again to be able to sleep again. Rinse and repeat.

I woke up at 11 am. In the garden. I thought: *I'm too pissed to drive to get some more plonk and, to be honest, I'm a bit too pissed to walk to the pub because I will only make a fool of myself. I'm already drunk and I am already crying before I've spoken to anybody.*

The people of Monkstone had been very kind and cuddled me for all they were worth, but what I needed were Bradford people and the Yorkshire form of TLC, but all my relations up there were dead. There was no-one left. Only Fred. My 'brother'.

Chapter Twenty-One
Fred Hubbard

I SENT a text to Fred. I don't know how many years it had been since I had seen him, or even spoken to him. I put: 'Help. I'm struggling.'

The phone pinged straight away. The reply was: 'Don't move. We'll be there in two hours.' I went back to sleep.

Fred and his wife Helen are very Yorkshire. Except they don't drink and they don't smoke. They don't swear. I am amazed they have had kids. They don't eat anything that doesn't come from the garden. They are boring as fuck. It was like Oliver Reid visiting the set of 'The Good Life'.

I am being very unfair. I have loved them both since the first moment that I met them.

They drove down from Bradford and woke me up, and we exchanged hugs – long, tearful ones from me. They then fed me, packed me into the back of their car, threw some clothes in carrier bags and drove me back to their house in Bradford where I was battered into shape over five days of the cruellest cold turkey known to man.

"I know that you are sad, TJ, but you are not here on holiday, and that washing up won't do itself," was the kindest gesture offered. At any stage of the five days, I would have happily sneaked out of the back door and walked the 90 miles home. But it was just what I needed, and I forced myself to stay.

I will never forget the first horrific night in their eldest daughter's old bedroom at the back of their creaking and draughty farmhouse up on the hills outside Bradford.

I didn't sleep a wink and couldn't settle in bed or the equally uncomfortable chair, and I didn't have a radio that I usually use to get me off to sleep.

I was whisky hungover. I had the feeling that I had lost or was certainly losing the only woman that I had truly loved, and I really felt that the loss of my beautiful daughter was the least of my worries.

I had only one consolation. At least I was one place off the rock bottom that I was at before I picked up the mobile phone at home that morning. Thank fuck we lived in a bungalow that didn't have bannisters.

Chapter Twenty-Two
Pop Goes the Alkie

I STILL go out. Pretty much every night, actually, but now I go to our nearest where Dubliner Declan makes me coffees while hiding a heart the size of the QE2 behind a gruff exterior, or down to the Green Dragon where I drink pop in the company of the wonderful Jason and his magnificent crew who ignore my occasional tears magnificently.

Not bad for someone who was a full-blown alkie for the best part of half a century.

I will never drink again, for the simple reason that it just did not suit me. I got to the stage where, following the death of Anna, I wasn't even getting drunk.

I wasn't getting that wonderful buzz of being on top of the world when you love everybody like in the initial stages of the Fairytale of New York. I was going straight to the stage where Kirsty was getting all cut up just singing about it.

(You just never know with sub-editors until you leave these things in, I reckon).

It was just going to enhance the black depression – whereas I found that without alcohol, I could speak much more succinctly about the problems that I was facing and could offer any help to those who may be seeking for it themselves.

I don't believe in counselling and all that, because I am one of those smart arses that knows all the answers, but if it works for you then crack on and ignore me.

It's just not for me, and I just use the opportunity to talk to a human as opposed to the wife, rather than get anything from it in terms of sorting out the mess that is generally going on in my head at any given time.

I have however heard that counselling is a great service, and one of my greatest and oldest friends tells me that his son has gained considerable solace and comfort from using the services of counsellors over his turbulent years. So, it's a case of don't knock it till you've tried it.

But I suppose if you argued a case long enough, you could strike up a point for anything. After all, someone voted for Boris.

I suppose you're wondering about the heroine of this story. The wonderful, long-suffering Maria is asleep in the other room because she gets it while she can.

When she's not lying awake staring at Anna's ashes and softly crying, she is looking after Ally Louise, who is going through teething at the moment, so Maria is being the Super Granny while Abbi is doing her damndest to try and raise two wonderful children while juggling hormones that are all over the place.

The first thing I did after we found the body amid all the police and paramedics was turn the car around and go back to Abbi and put my arm round her.

"I know the loss of your sister will haunt you for ever, but please realise that when people are contemplating suicide they are not thinking like normal people are – they are only looking at the end result," I said.

"Otherwise Anna wouldn't have done that because she loved you so much. Please believe me."

Sometimes it's as tough being a dad as it is being an orphan.

I've spent a career looking for words to get me out of tight situations, and the fact that I have had very few fights suggests that it has worked so far. In fact that only time that a punch was thrown at me in Monkstone (at least, before this book was released) the bloke was so pissed I had time to drink up and leave before it had landed.

Chapter Twenty-Three
Gramps

AFTER being a self-confessed crap dad, I feel completely justified in claiming to be a world-class grandad. Although I am not called that. I am known as 'Gramps'.

Jenny is hilarious and we play for hours together, and a fine example of how we get on came on the first occasion that she stayed over lately.

We played all evening, and then she watched some videos with Maria on the couch in the lounge before climbing into Maria's double bed and demanding that Gramps reads her five books before she can go to sleep.

So I start off reading and she pretends to go to sleep but, after three books, we notice that Granny has actually gone to sleep first.

This is a good thing, because she's not had a lot of sleep in six months, bless her. When she sleeps she is more rational, but you still have to tread on eggshells around her.

Eventually Jenny nestles into her, and she falls asleep as well. And as I look over them together, next to them on the table is Anna's ashes, looking over them as well.

I was worried when Maria and I brought the ashes home together, because she is not as the same stage of acceptance that I have arrived at.

The long-wave radio reception is still flickering. Maria is still drinking and crying herself to sleep, and if she needs to do that at this stage, then that is fine.

I asked her what she was going to do with the ashes, whether she was going to bury them, scatter them, or what. She just said simply: "I'm going to put them next to the bed."

I shouted: "Are you crazy, woman? Are you completely mad? What in God's name can you possibly be thinking of? I've bloody well seen it all now!! Good God above!!!"

But I didn't say it out loud, like I would have done if I had had a drink or six. I just said gently: "Okay, love." And there they are.

When Maria is out, I wander through to her bedroom and sit on the edge of bed, and Anna and I chat for a while. Not for long, because I know that would piss her off, but just long enough to let her know that I love her, and understand that she did what she did, and why she had to do it.

And I tell her that I hope that God is looking after her and that He has turned out to be everything that I've always hoped that He would be. And she listens and she smiles. There's no laughter at those times – just a peaceful understanding.

The other morning I was getting ready to go to my mate's to set off for a football match, and I walked past the bedroom door and said: "Alright, love?"

And I'm sure I sensed Anna's cheeky voice of old say: "Yeah, apart from dead, twat!"

Chapter Twenty-Four
The Happy Ending?

MARIA and I are now retired; well, she's a full-time grandma and I'm a grandfather who does his best to try and love everyone and cope with being surrounded by social hand grenades (you never know when they're going to go off).

The rest of the time Maria does her best for everyone, tries to mend herself with sleep, and tries to shoulder the burden of her crushing pain as best as she can. And I do what I'm told to do most of the time.

I love her more than I did when I walked into that classroom at Darlington 40 years ago, because she is now not just sex on a stick.

I've seen her love and care for the people of Monkstone through her years at the local paper, through her time doing voluntary work at the hospital in the town, and I've seen her steer and guide and nourish her children in a way that is a magnificent example to all women and mothers everywhere.

I've been a recipient of that love far more than I have deserved, and I dedicate all the words in this book to her with all my heart.

But I have also seen that love now transferred to two little girls that do not know now what a magnificent world is awaiting them in her company in the next few years to come.

Maria is astonishing, and I hope for our grandchildren's sake and for all of us that she lives to a ripe old age. God knows that her mother did (I thought it was going to take green Kryptonite in the end, to be honest).

I remember when Ally was born, and when I held her it felt all wrong. It was only a few days after Anna had hanged herself, and it was just cruelly wrong.

It sounds horrible to say it – but until I started writing this book I didn't expect to be pouring out my heart to you right from the very bottom of my soul, because I now know what it feels like to have been thoroughly dredged – but Ally was just like a substitute, and it took a bit of time to warm to her. Which is something that a grandfather should not have in his locker.

But you have to adjust and you have to cope with these things, because life isn't designed to be a piece of piss whatever level you're at. It's a challenge.

At the christening Abbi told me that her new baby was going to be called Ally Louise, because Louise had been Anna's middle name.

I said that I could obviously understand the sentiment and the reasoning behind that but added that, from my point of view, I would have appreciated it if she had been given the middle name 'McCoist' because he had been a fine footballer in his day and did a great job on the Talk Sport breakfast show.

But apparently 'Sod off, dad' means 'no'. So there you go. You just can't help some people.

When your world comes to a crashing end with something like the death of your daughter – and to me a hanging seems to be the most horrific of things that can happen to a family – people come out with all sorts of lines that are well-meaning and intended to make you feel better. And the most heard one, the most popular, is: 'Time is a great healer.'

That is because it is. Time is a great healer. And God puts up with all the shit that you throw at him, and He is there tomorrow, just waiting round the corner, ready to see if you have calmed down and want to chat again.

And I always do, because we walk together. It's what we do, and I would be lost and lonely without him. There may well be time for me to be a priest yet.

If you heard a loud bang just then, don't worry. It was just someone dropping a book in the Vatican.

It's like when you have loved someone for 40 years. You don't just say: "Oh, bollocks to you, then. You're not the person I married; you're not the person I fell in love with all those years ago."

They are. You just have to wait till that person comes back around again. Like God does. If you've waited 40 years, what's a bit longer?

The modern world is too ready to write things off, too ready to dismiss things. If I sound like an old git, then I am proud to be one. I have learned far more about life in three years as a grandfather than I ever did than I ever did in 43 years as a journalist.

And not drinking has changed my life around more than I ever thought possible. I now love the simple things, like a child's wonder when you blow a bubble with that washing up liquid stuff that you can buy in tubes.

Jenny's face as the bubble climbs high in the sky is enchanting. Sometimes the bubble goes right over our house. Okay, we live in a bungalow. Piss right off.

And Ally has started to watch her reactions, and she smiles when Jenny smiles. And that makes Granny and Gramps smile too. And that is called mending. Thank you, God.